PIANO | VOCAL | GUITAR • CD

VOLUME 123

HAL•LEONARD

Piano Play-Along

CHRIS TOMLIN

ISBN 978-1-4584-2449-5

HAL•LEONARD®
CORPORATION

7777 W. BLUEMOUND RD. P.O. BOX 13819 MILWAUKEE, WI 53213

Visit Hal Leonard Online at
www.halleonard.com

AMAZING GRACE
(My Chains Are Gone)

Words by JOHN NEWTON
Traditional American Melody
Additional Words and Music by CHRIS TOMLIN
and LOUIE GIGLIO

Gently

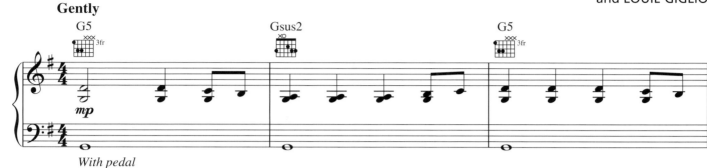

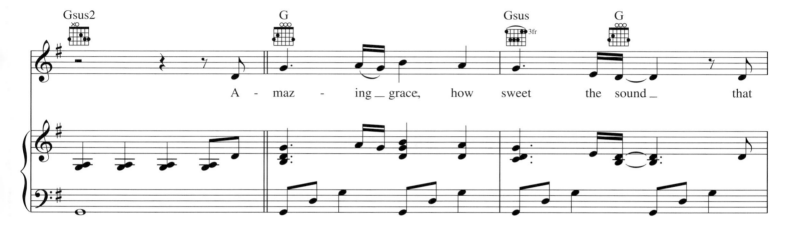

A-maz-ing grace, how sweet the sound that

saved a wretch like me. I once was lost but

now I'm found, was blind but now I see. 'Twas

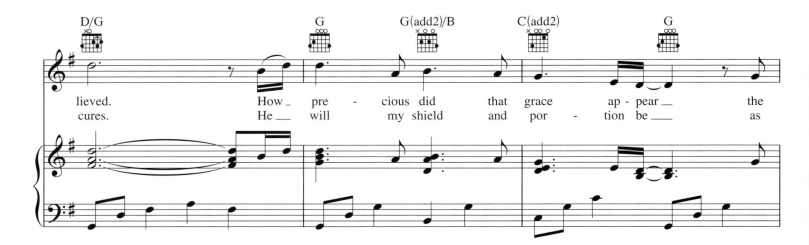

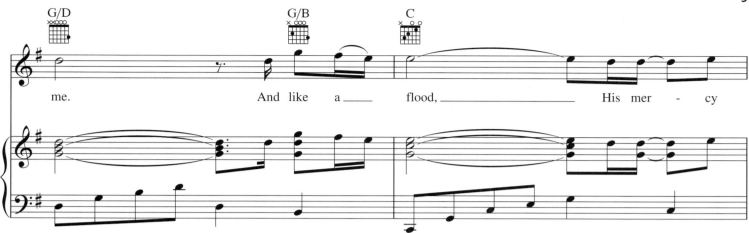

me. And like a ___ flood, _____ His mer - cy

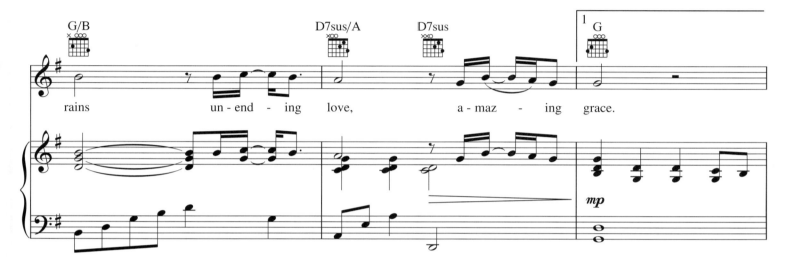

rains un - end - ing love, a - maz - ing grace.

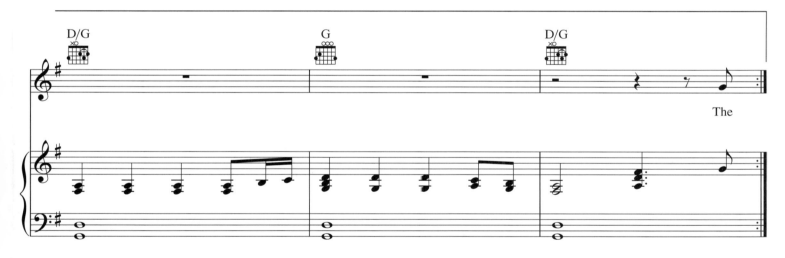

The

grace. My chains are gone, I've been set ___ free. My God, my

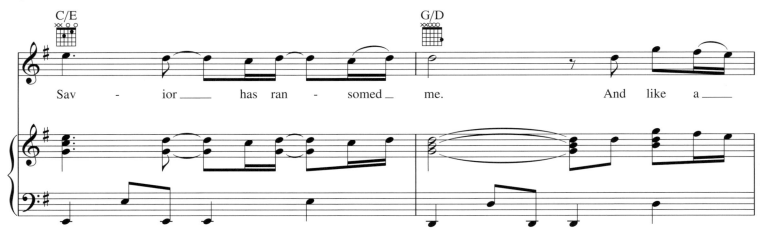

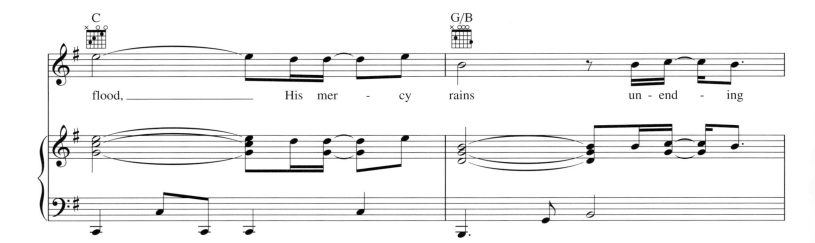

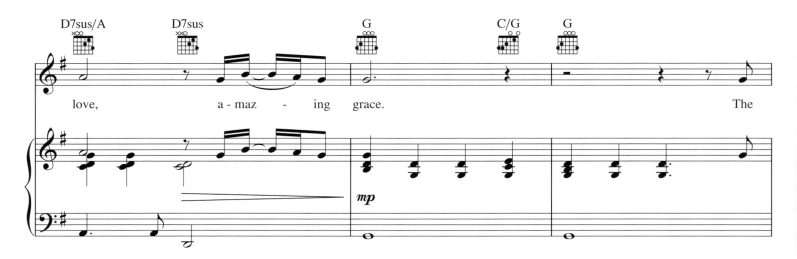

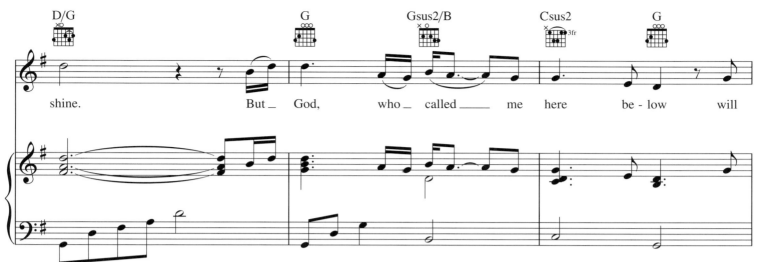

shine.　　But __ God,　who __ called _____ me　here　be - low　will

be　for - ev - er　mine,　　will　be　for - ev - er

mine.　　You　are　for - ev - er　mine.

HOLY IS THE LORD

Words and Music by CHRIS TOMLIN
and LOUIE GIGLIO

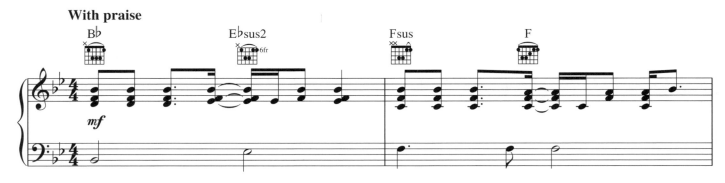

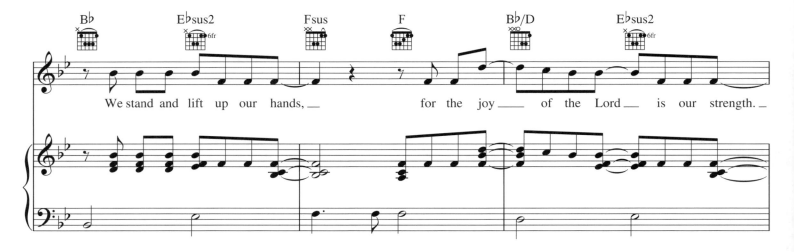

We stand and lift up our hands, __ for the joy __ of the Lord __ is our strength. __

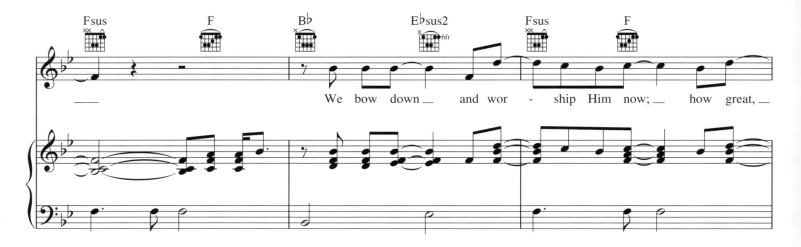

__ We bow down __ and wor - ship Him now; __ how great, __

_how awe - some is He. ___ And to - geth - er we ___ sing: ___

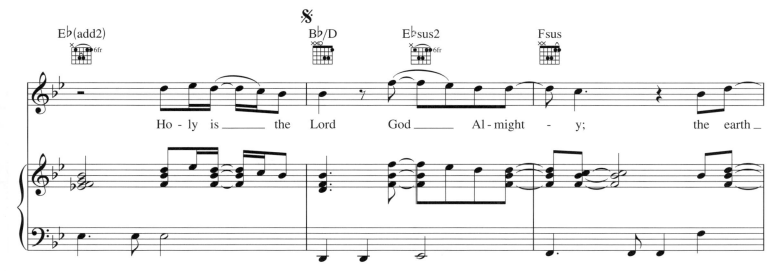

Ho - ly is ___ the Lord God ___ Al - might - y; ___ the earth _

___ is filled _ with His glo - ry. Ho - ly is ___ the Lord God ___ Al - might-

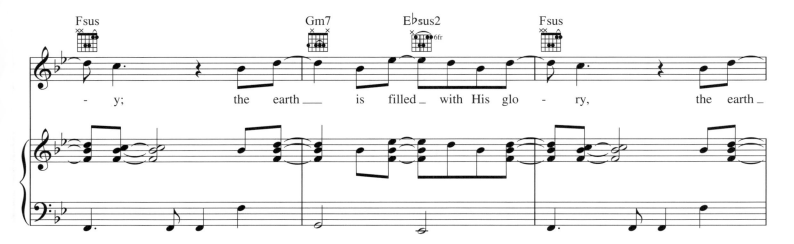

- y; ___ the earth ___ is filled _ with His glo - ry, ___ the earth _

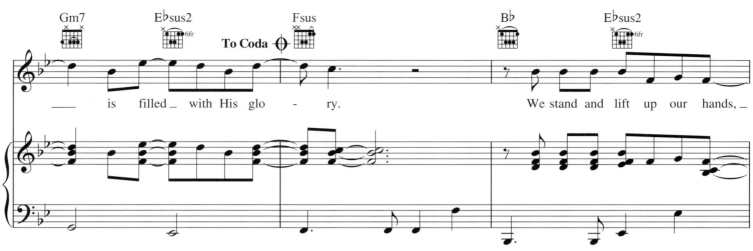

is filled __ with His glo - ry. We stand and lift up our hands, __

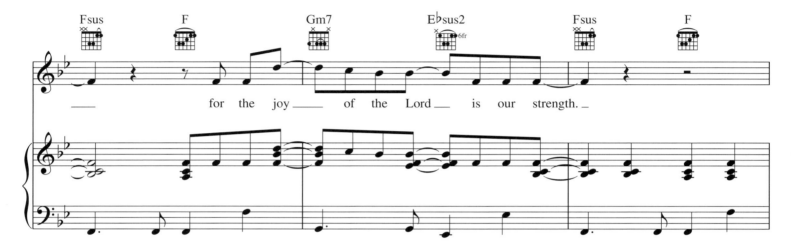

__ for the joy ____ of the Lord __ is our strength. __

We bow down __ and wor - ship Him now; __ how great, __ how awe - some is He. __

__ And to - geth - er we __ sing, __ ev - 'ry - one

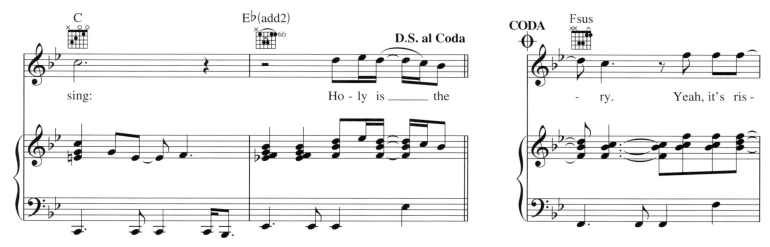

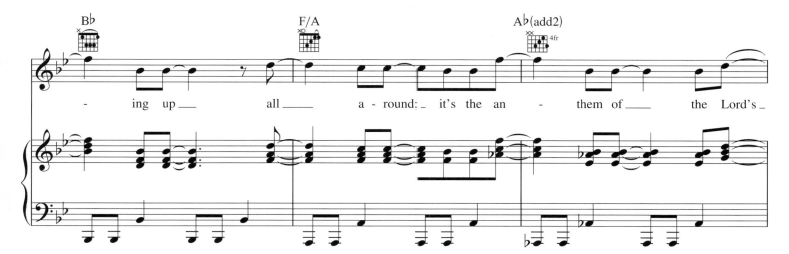

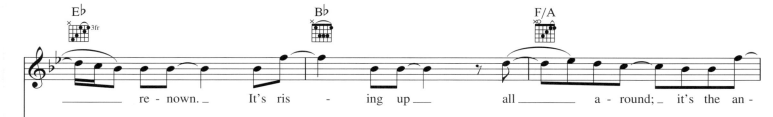

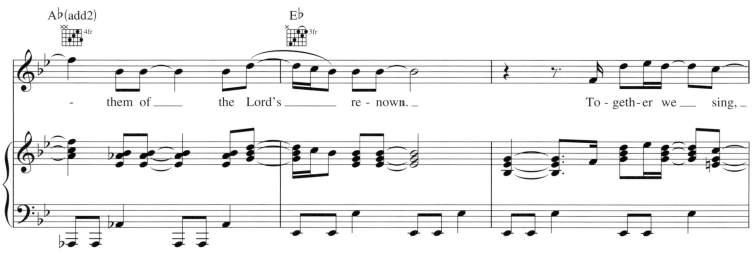

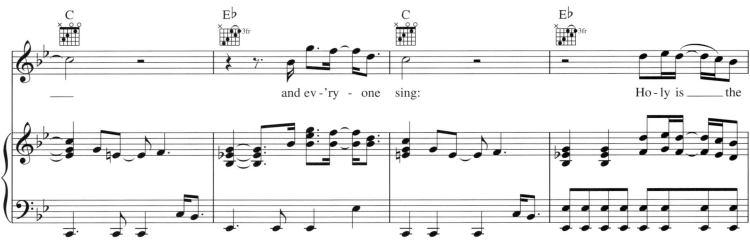

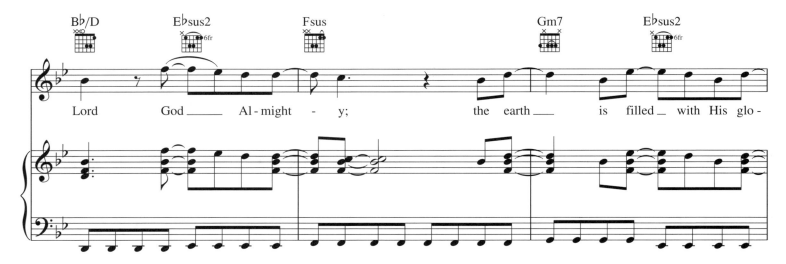

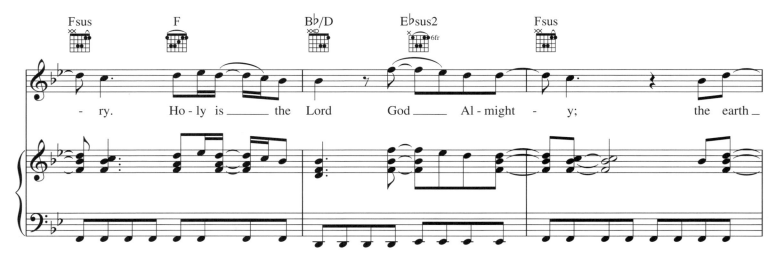

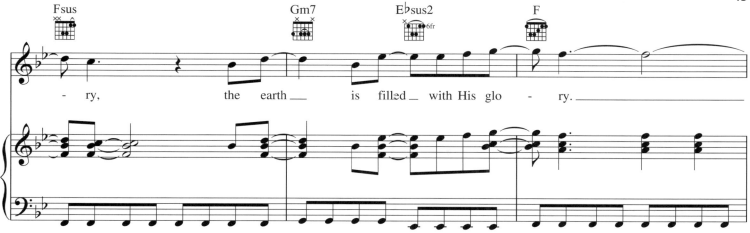

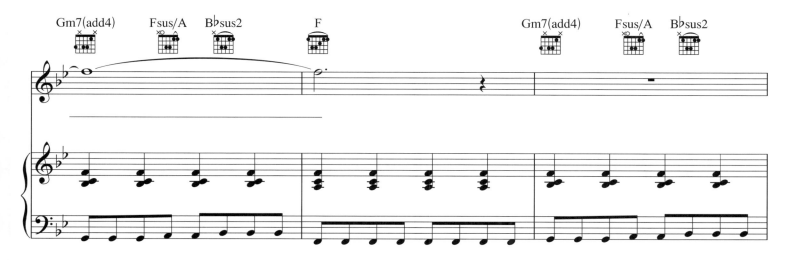

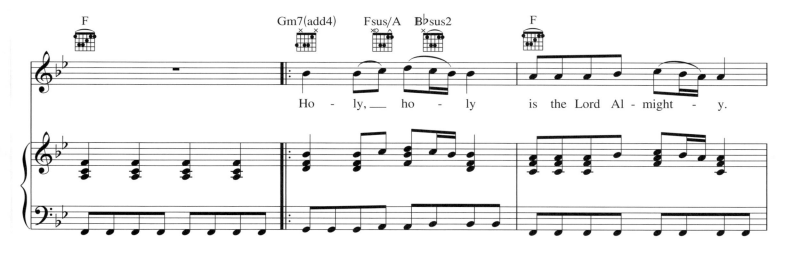

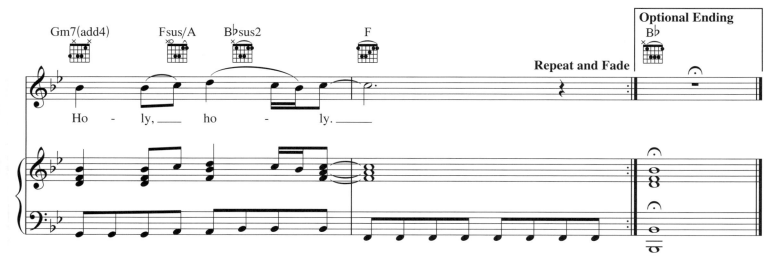

HOW GREAT IS OUR GOD

Words and Music by CHRIS TOMLIN,
JESSE REEVES and ED CASH

With praise

The splen - dor of ___ a King, ___ and
age to age ___ He stands, ___

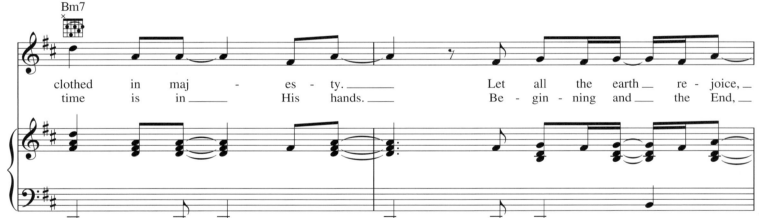

clothed in maj - es - ty. ___ Let all the earth ___ re - joice, ___
time is in ___ His hands. ___ Be - gin - ning and ___ the End, ___

___ all the earth ___ re - joice. ___ He wraps ___ Him - self ___ in light, ___
___ Be - gin - ning and ___ the End. ___ The God - head, Three ___ in One, ___

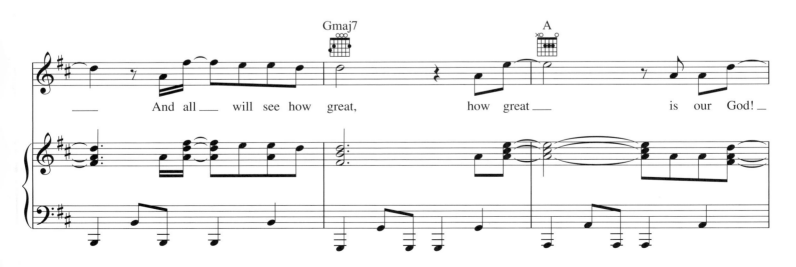

How great ___ is our God! ___

Sing with me: ___ How great is our God! ___

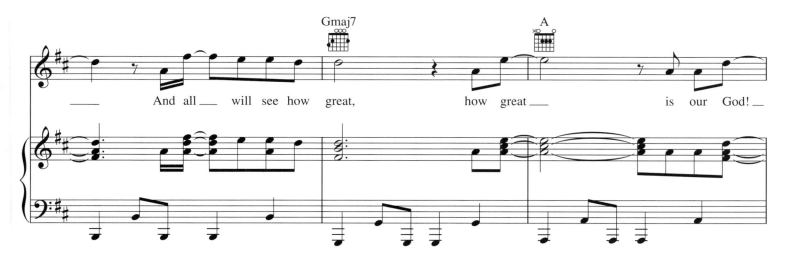

___ And all ___ will see how great, how great ___ is our God! ___

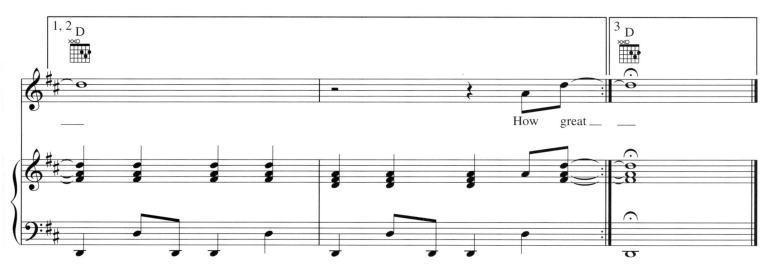

How great ___

I LIFT MY HANDS

Words and Music by CHRIS TOMLIN,
LOUIE GIGLIO and MATT MAHER

a for-tress for the weak. ___
that wash-es o-ver me. ___
Let faith a - rise, ___

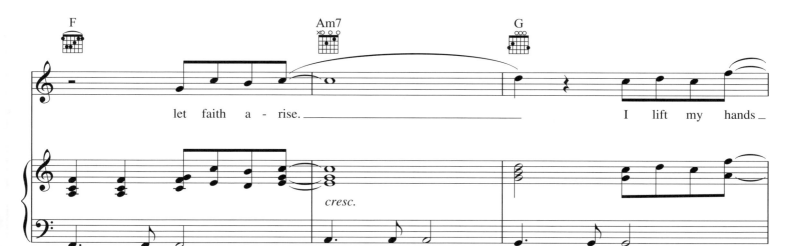

let faith a - rise. ___ I lift my hands ___

___ to be-lieve ___ a - gain. You are my ref - uge, ___ You ___ are my strength. ___

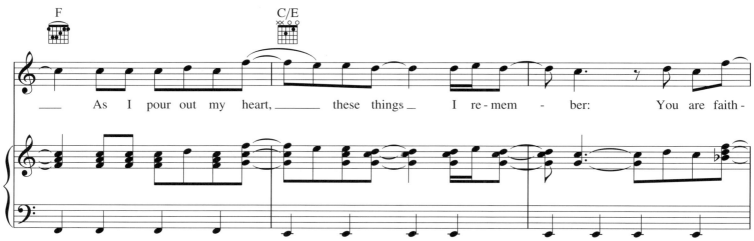

___ As I pour out my heart, ___ these things ___ I re-mem - ber: You are faith-

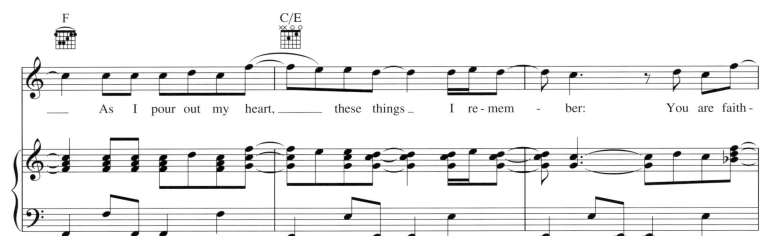

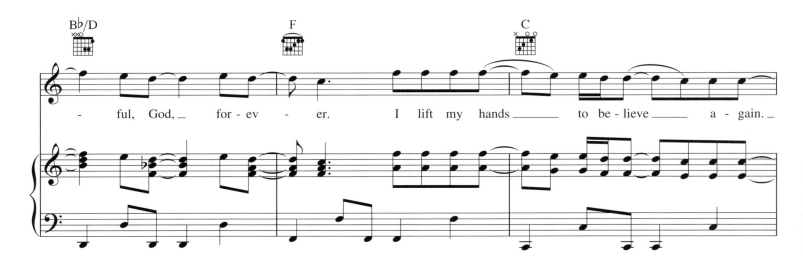

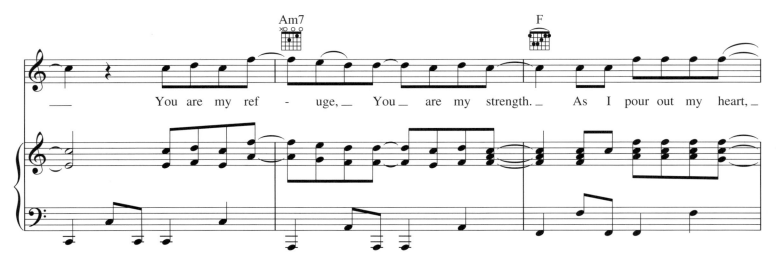

these things __ I re-mem - ber: You are faith - ful, God, __ You're faith-

- ful, God, __ for - ev - er. _____

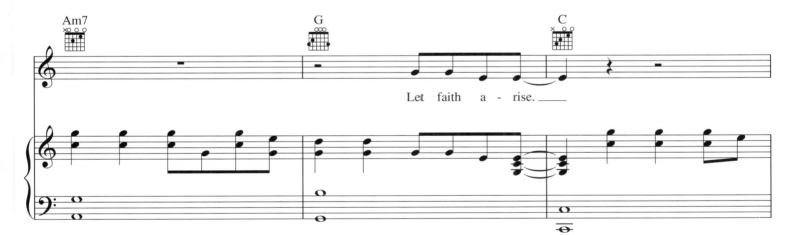

Let faith a - rise. _____

Let faith a - rise. _____

I WILL RISE

Words and Music by CHRIS TOMLIN,
JESSE REEVES, LOUIE GIGLIO
and MATT MAHER

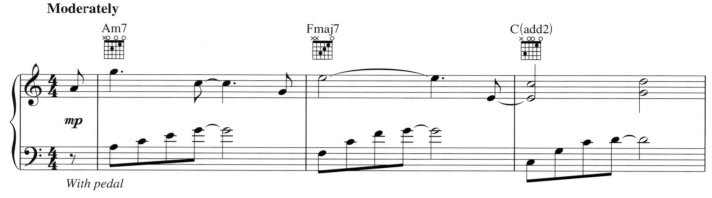

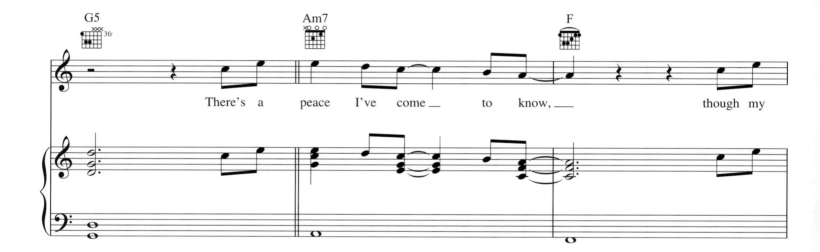

There's a peace I've come ___ to know, ___ though my

heart and flesh ___ may fail. ___ There's an an - chor for ___ my soul. ___

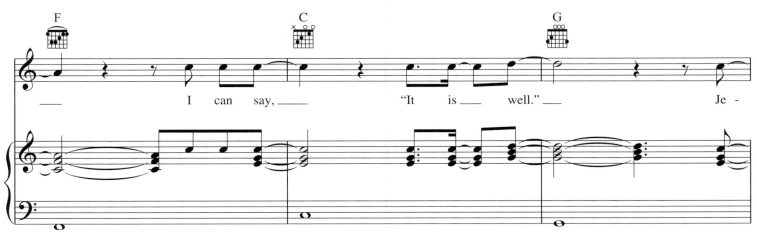

I can say, ___ "It is ___ well." ___ Je-

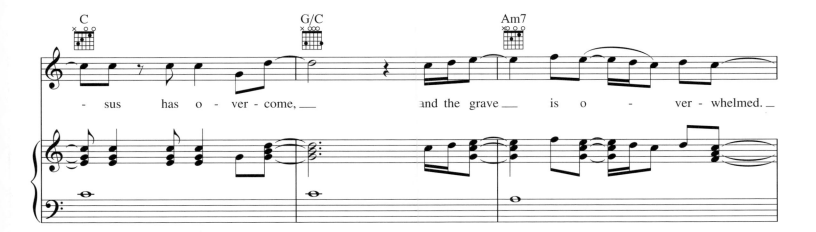

-sus has o-ver-come, ___ and the grave ___ is o-ver-whelmed. ___

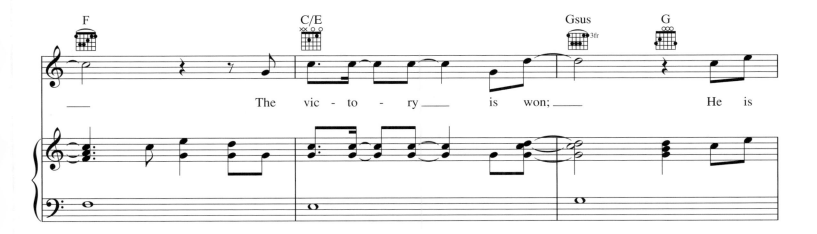

___ The vic-to-ry ___ is won; ___ He is

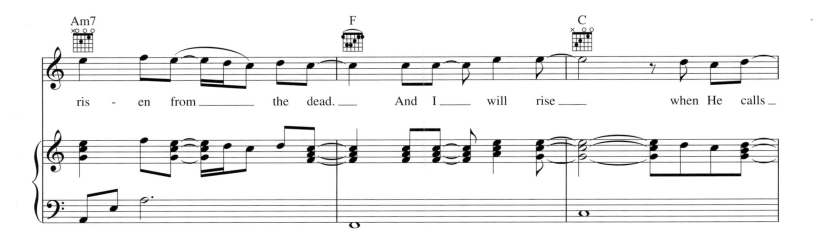

ris-en from ___ the dead. ___ And I ___ will rise ___ when He calls ___

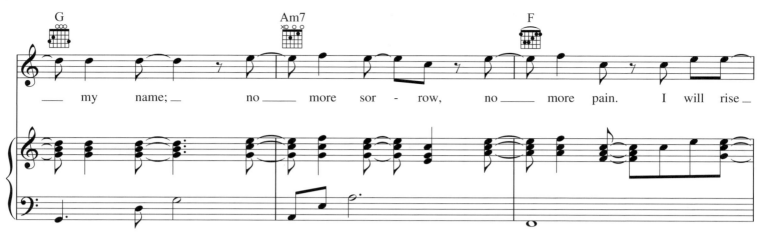

____ my name; ____ no ____ more sor - row, no ____ more pain. I will rise ____

____ on ea - gles' wings, ____ be - fore ____ my God ____ fall on ____

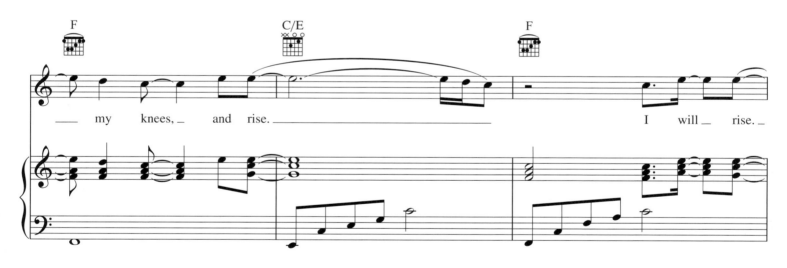

____ my knees, ____ and rise. _____ I will ____ rise. ____

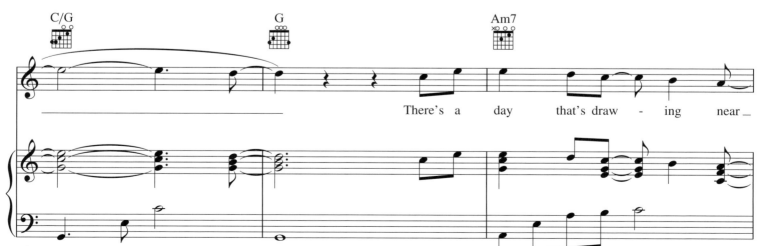

_____ There's a day that's draw - ing near ____

when this dark - ness breaks __ to light, __ and the

shad - ows dis - ap - pear, __ and my faith __ shall be __ my eyes. __

Je - sus has o - ver-come, __ and the grave __

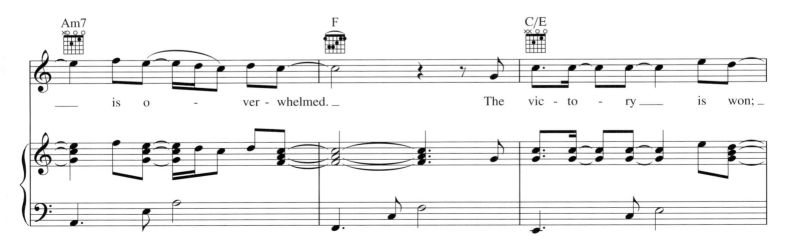

is o - ver-whelmed. __ The vic - to - ry __ is won; __

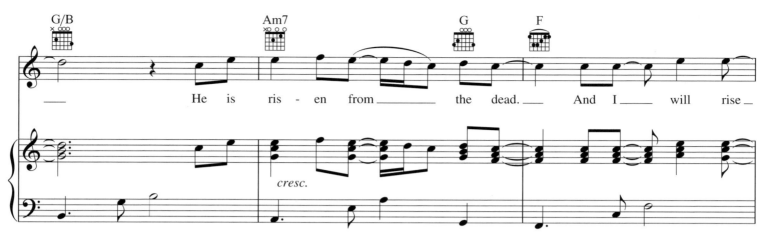

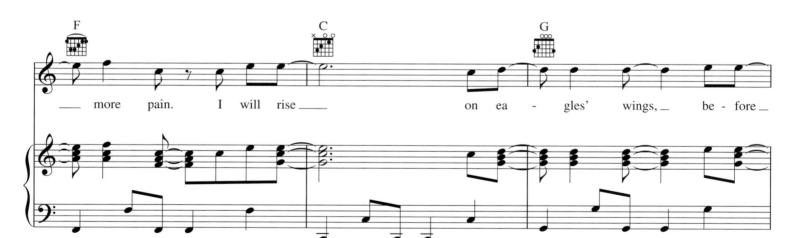

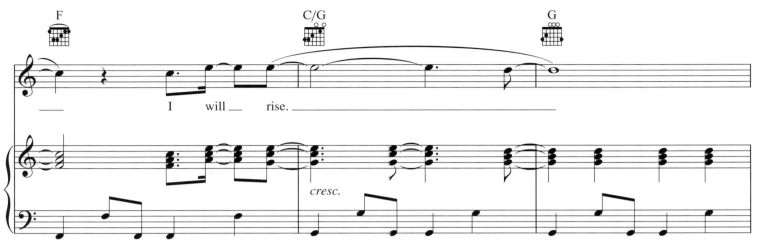

I will __ rise. __

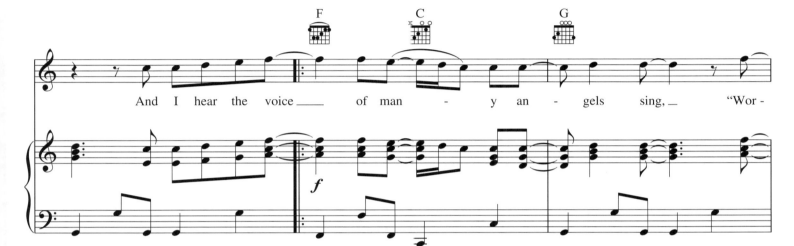

And I hear the voice __ of man - y an - gels sing, __ "Wor -

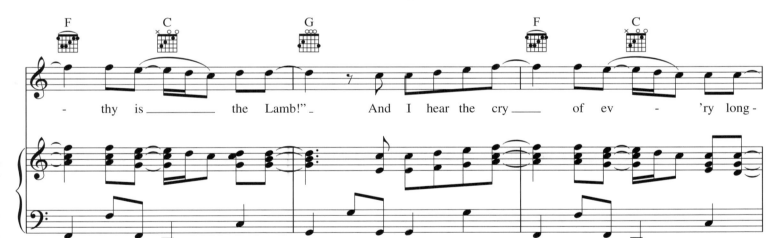

- thy is _____ the Lamb!" __ And I hear the cry __ of ev - 'ry long -

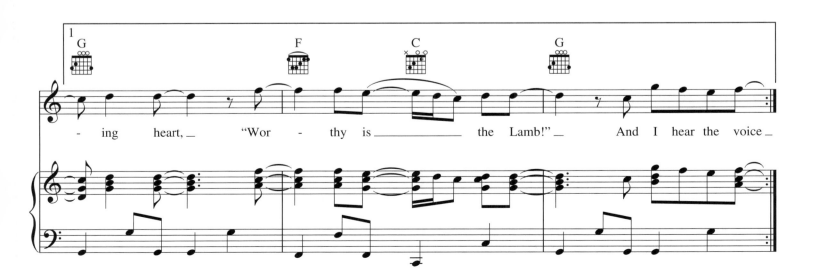

- ing heart, __ "Wor - thy is _____ the Lamb!" __ And I hear the voice __

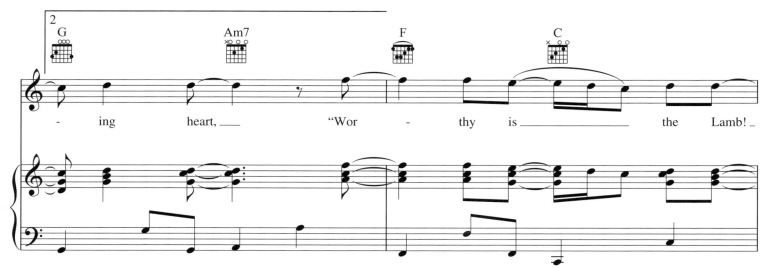

-ing heart, ____ "Wor - thy is _____ the Lamb! _

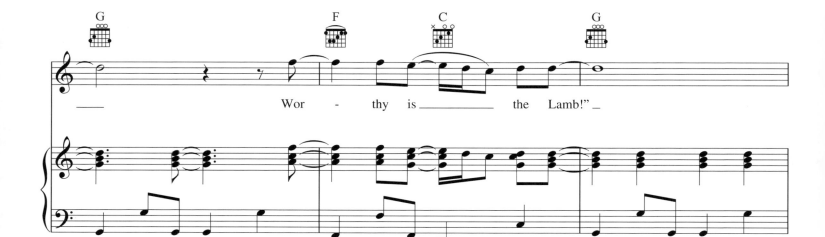

____ Wor - thy is _____ the Lamb!" _

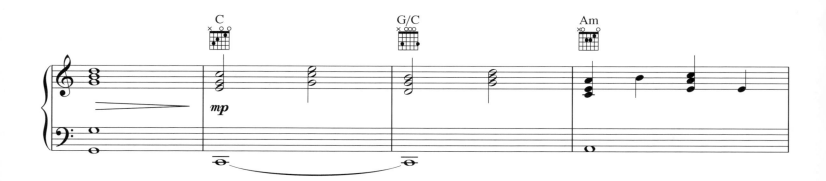

I will ___ rise _____ when He calls ___ my name; no ___

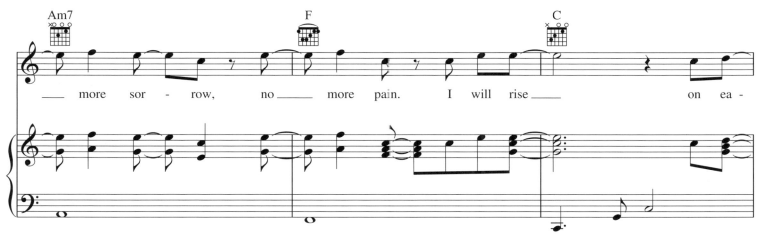

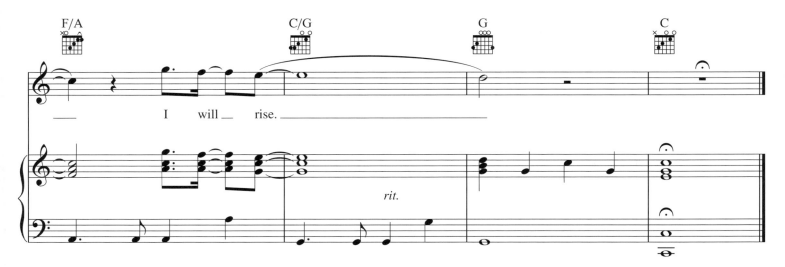

JESUS MESSIAH

Words and Music by CHRIS TOMLIN,
JESSE REEVES, DANIEL CARSON
and ED CASH

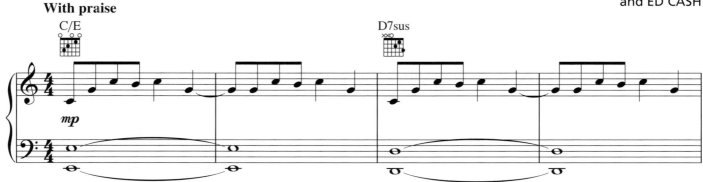

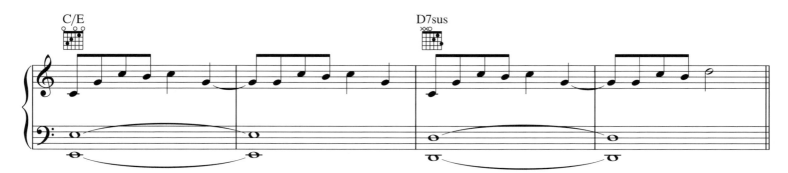

He be-came_ sin_ who knew no_ sin,_ that we might be-come_ His_

_ right-eous-ness. He hum-bled Him-self_ and car-ried the_ cross._

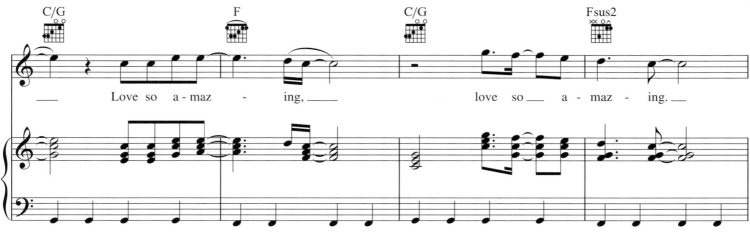

Love so a - maz - ing, ____ love so a - maz - ing.

Je - sus Mes - si - ah, ____ Name a - bove all ____

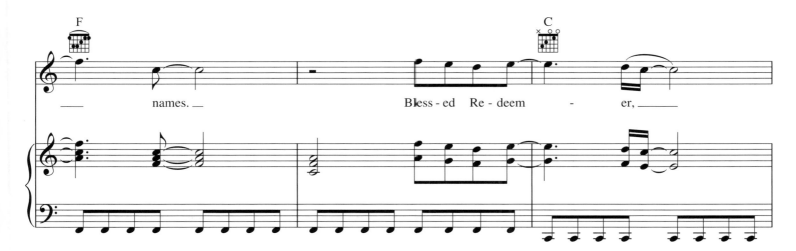

____ names. ____ Bless - ed Re - deem - er, ____

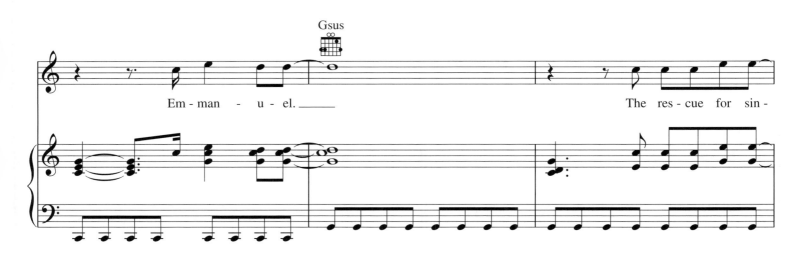

Em - man - u - el. ____ The res - cue for sin -

34

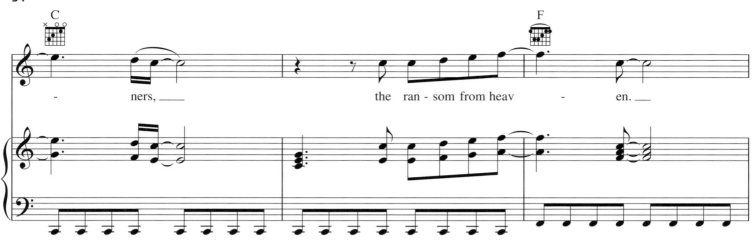

-ners, _____ the ran-som from heav - en. _____

Je - sus Mes - si - ah, _____ Lord of all. _____

To Coda

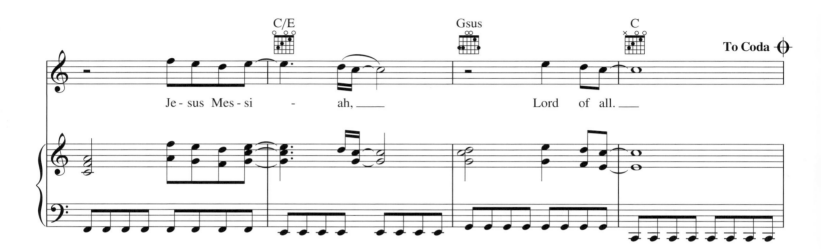

His bod - y the _ bread, _ His blood the _ wine, _

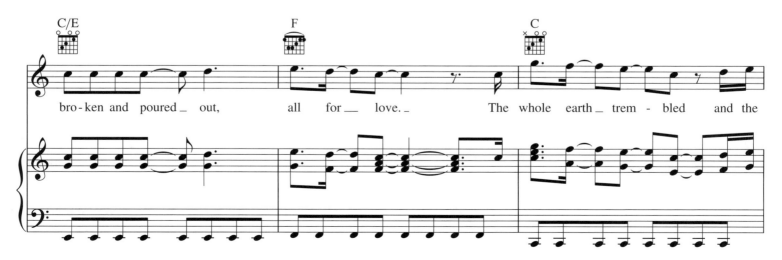

bro-ken and poured _ out, all for _ love. _ The whole earth _ trem - bled and the

veil was __ torn. _____ Love so a - maz - - ing, ____

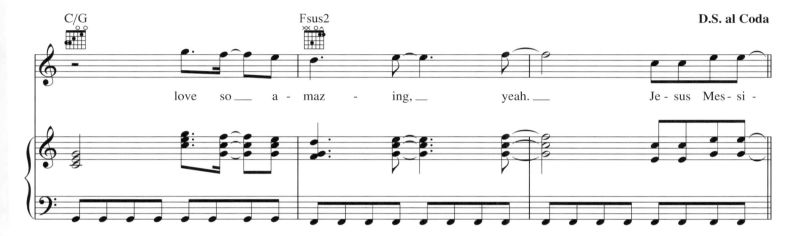

love so __ a - maz - - ing, __ yeah. __ Je - sus Mes - si -

D.S. al Coda

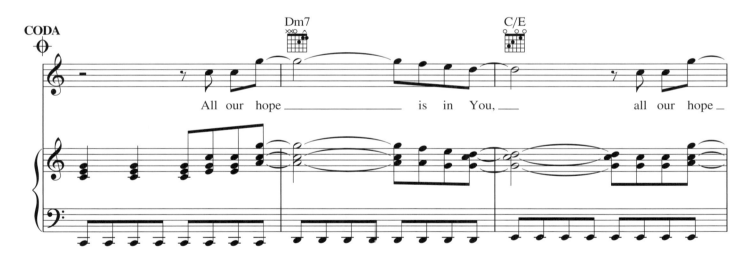

CODA

All our hope _____ is in You, ___ all our hope __

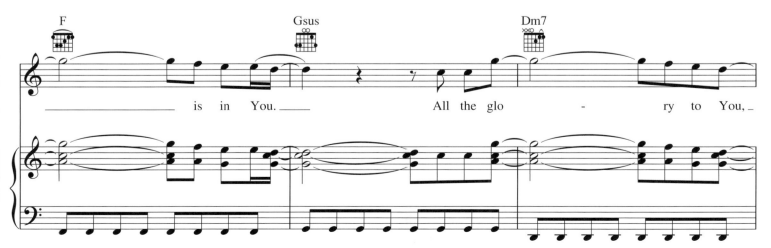

_____ is in You. ____ All the glo - - ry to You, _

God, ____ the Light of __ the __ world. _____

Je - sus, Mes - si - ah, _____ Name a - bove all ____ names. _

Bless-ed Re-deem - er, ____ Em - man - u - el. ____

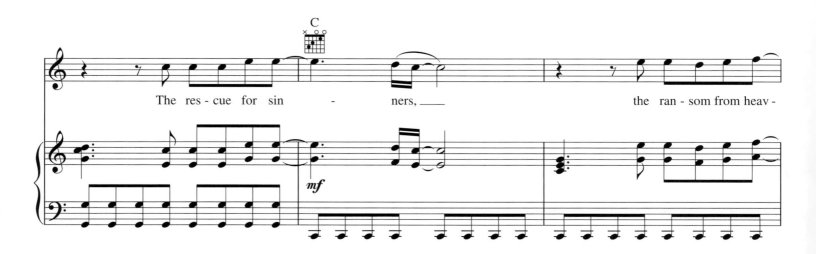

The res - cue for sin - ners, ____ the ran - som from heav-

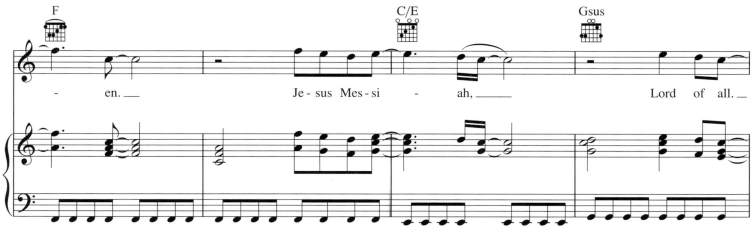

OUR GOD

Words and Music by JONAS MYRIN,
CHRIS TOMLIN, MATT REDMAN
and JESSE REEVES

With power

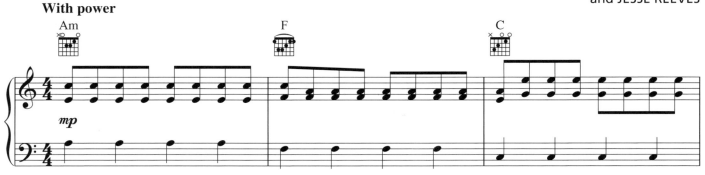

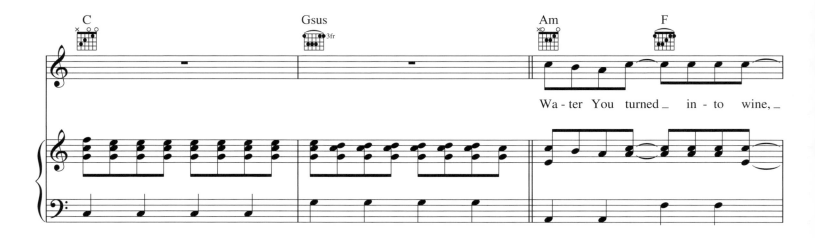

Wa- ter You turned __ in- to wine, __

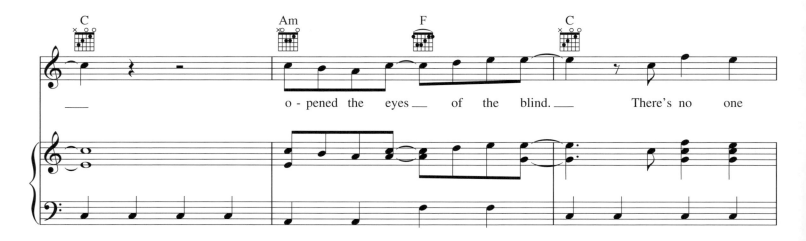

__ o- pened the eyes __ of the blind. __ There's no one

like You, ____ none like _____ You. _____

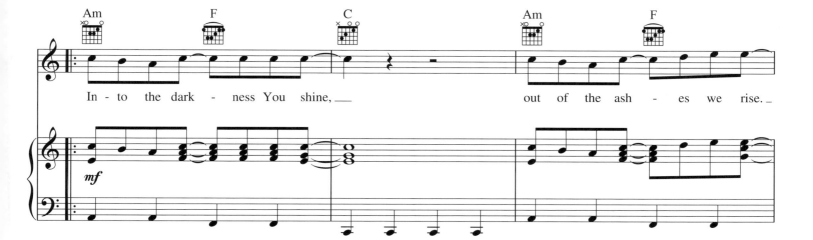

In - to the dark - ness You shine, ___ out of the ash - es we rise. ___

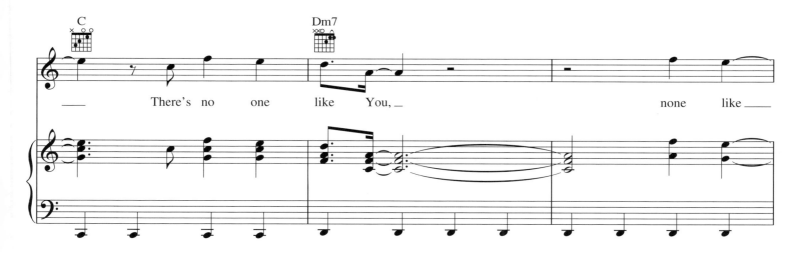

____ There's no one like You, ___ none like ____

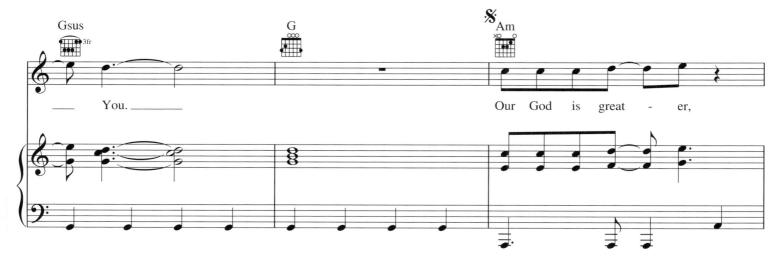

____ You. _____ Our God is great - er,

our God is strong - er. God, You are high - er than an - y oth - er.

Our God is Heal - er, awe - some in pow - er, our God, our God.

To Coda ⊕

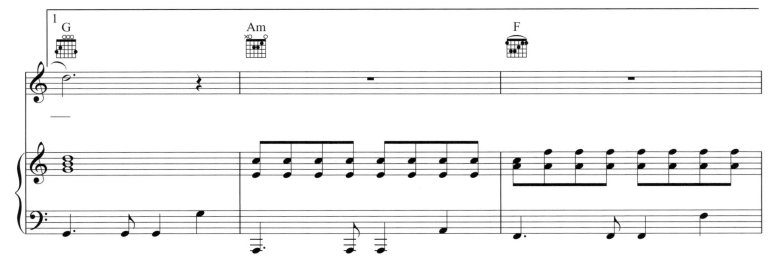

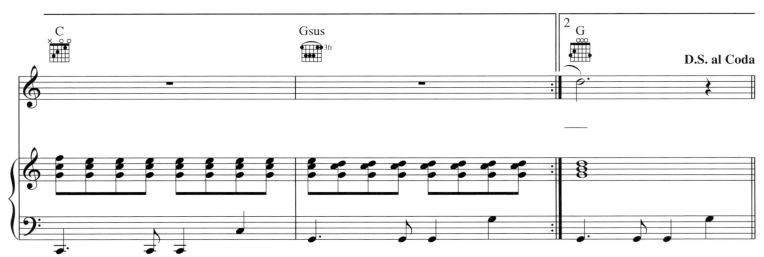

D.S. al Coda

CODA

gradual cresc.

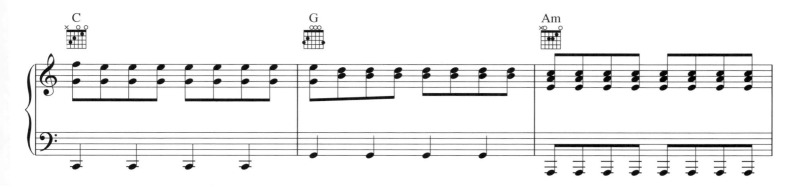

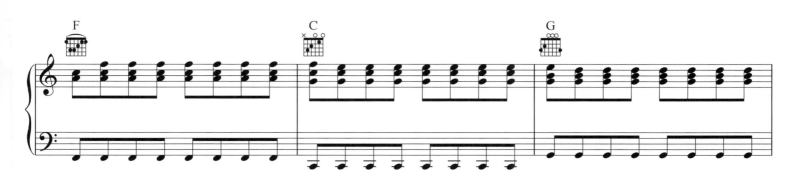

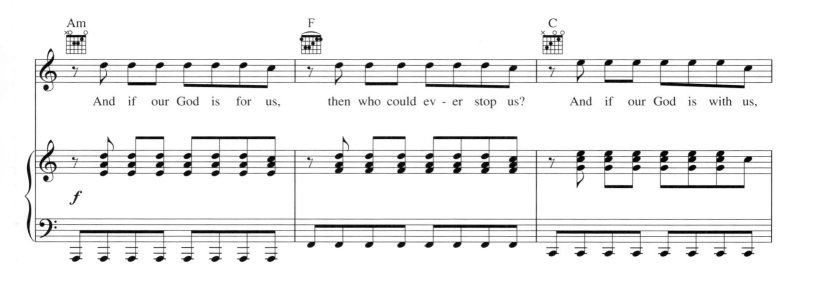

And if our God is for us, then who could ev - er stop us? And if our God is with us,

then what could stand a - gainst? _ And if our God is for us, then who could ev - er stop us?

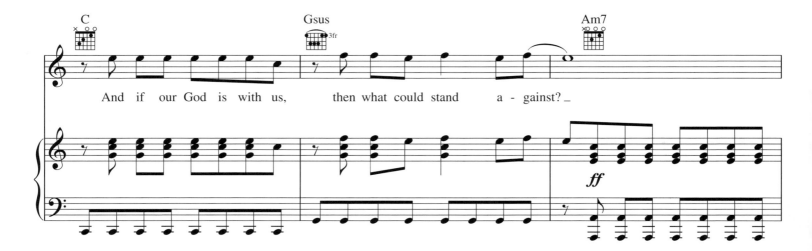

And if our God is with us, then what could stand a - gainst? _

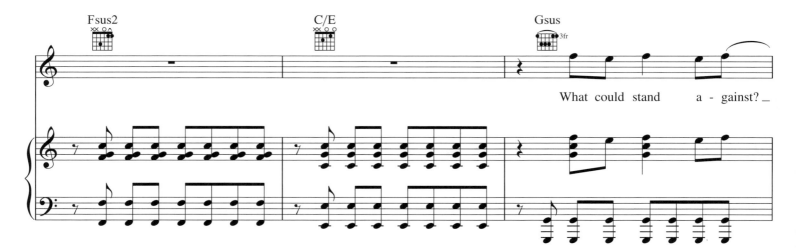

What could stand a - gainst? _

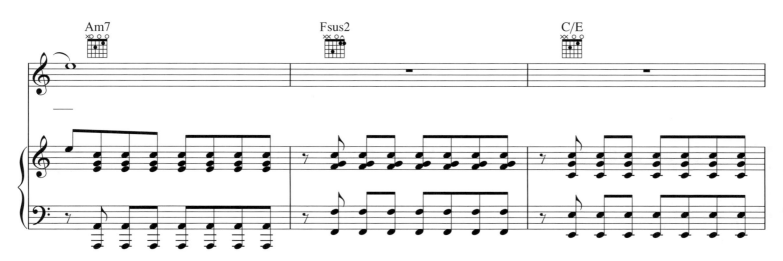

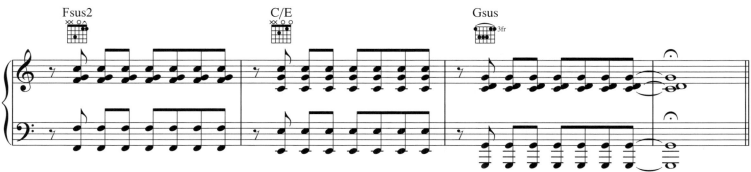

Our God is great - er, our God is strong - er. God, You are high - er than an -

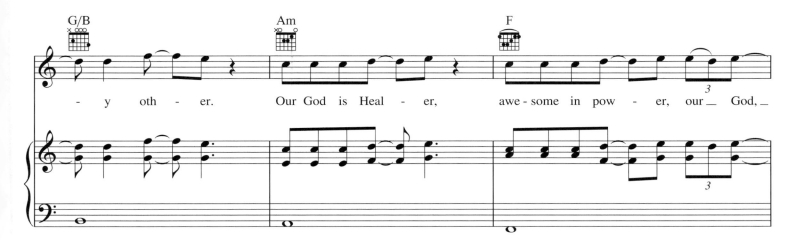

- y oth - er. Our God is Heal - er, awe - some in pow - er, our __ God, __

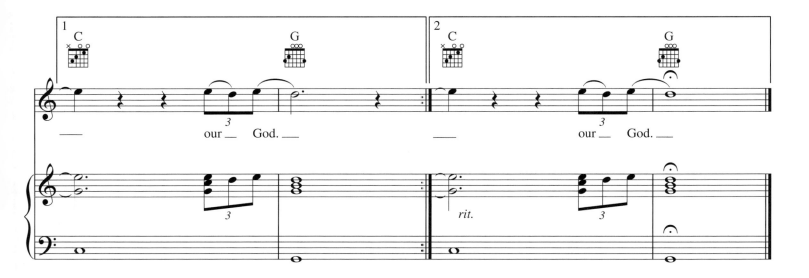

1 __ our __ God. __

2 __ our __ God. __

WE FALL DOWN

Words and Music by
CHRIS TOMLIN

Worshipfully

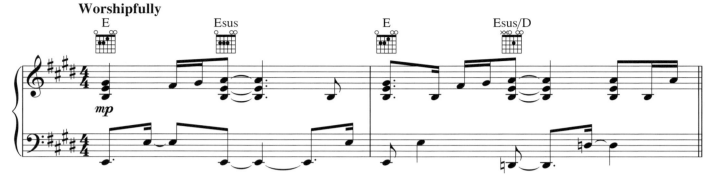

We fall __ down, __ we lay our __ crowns __ at the feet __ of Je-

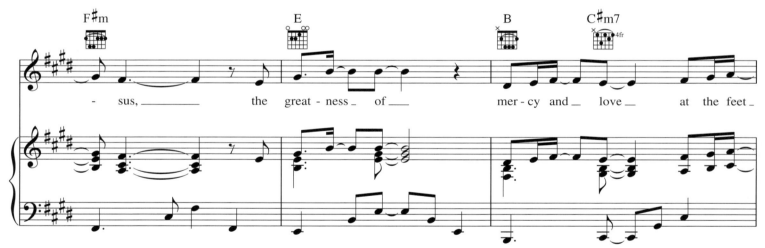

-sus, ___ the great-ness __ of __ mer-cy and __ love __ at the feet __

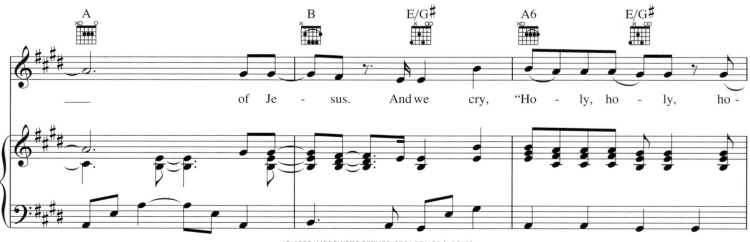

___ of Je - sus. And we cry, "Ho - ly, ho - ly, ho-

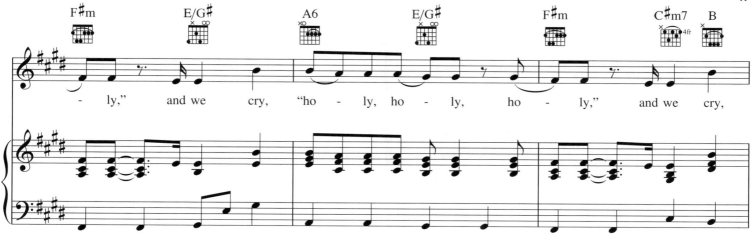

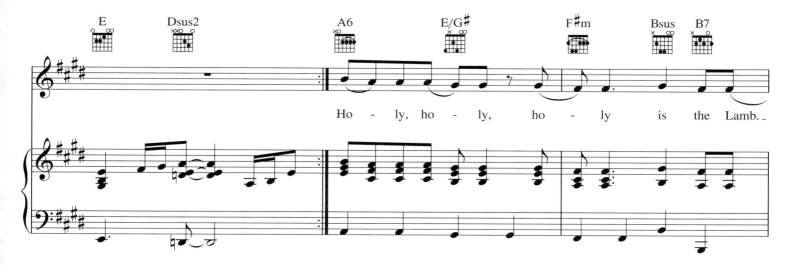

THE ULTIMATE SONGBOOKS

PIANO PLAY-ALONG

These great songbook/CD packs come with our standard arrangements for piano and voice with guitar chord frames plus a CD.

The CD includes a full performance of each song, as well as a second track without the piano part so you can play "lead" with the band!

HAL•LEONARD® CORPORATION
7777 W. Bluemound Rd. P.O. Box 13819
Milwaukee, Wisconsin 53213

Visit Hal Leonard Online at
www.halleonard.com

Prices, contents and availability subject to change without notice.
Disney characters and artwork © Disney Enterprises, Inc.